INSPIR LIVES

TIM BERNERS-LEE

CREATOR OF THE WEB

Claudia Martin

WAYLAND

Updated and published in paperback in 2017 by Wayland

Copyright © Hodder & Stoughton Limited, 2017

Wayland is an imprint of
Hachette Children's Group
Part of Hodder & Stoughton
Carmelite House, 50 Victoria Embankment
London EC4Y 0DZ

Produced for Wayland by
White-Thomson Publishing Ltd
www.wtpub.co.uk
+44 (0)843 208 7460

Editor: Claudia Martin
Design: Tim Mayer (Mayer Media)
Proofreader and indexer: Izzi Howell

A catalogue record for this title is available from the British Library.

ISBN: 978 0 7502 9313 6
Library ebook ISBN: 978 0 7502 9013 5
Dewey Number: 004'.092-dc23

Printed in China

10 9 8 7 6 5 4 3 2 1

Wayland is a division of Hachette
Children's Group, an Hachette UK
company.
www.hachette.co.uk

Picture acknowledgements:
The author and publisher would like to thank the following for allowing their pictures to be reproduced in this publication.
Badgerm: 7; **CERN:** 17, 19, 20, 21t, 22; **Corbis:** cover (Rick Friedman), 4 (Jason Florio), 6 (Bettmann); **Donna Coveney/MIT News Office/W3C:** 16; **Dreamstime:** 5 (Drserg), 13t (Tomd), 15 (Xdrew), 24 (Mircea Maties), 29 (Goodluz); **Emanuel School:** 11; **Getty Images:** 9, 23 (AFP), 26l (AFP), 26r (Dave M. Benett), 28 (AFP); **Hannes Grobe:** 13b; **Magdalena Krohn:** 18; **Robert Scoble:** 21b; **Shutterstock:** 8 (Bikeworldtravel); **Simononly:** 12; **Superstock:** 10 (Transtock), 25 (Hank Morgan/Rainbow); **Pablo Valerio:** 27; **Steven Walling:** 14.

Contents

'This is for everyone'

On 27 July 2012 a man sat in the centre of London's Olympic Stadium, typing at an old-fashioned computer. Across the world, 900 million people watched on their TVs. The man was Tim Berners-Lee and this was the opening ceremony of the Olympic Games. He sent a **tweet**: 'This is for everyone'. The message flashed up around the stadium.

Most of us check our favourite **websites** every day: we link up with friends, watch music videos or discover what's happening around the world. Whenever we use a website, we are using the **World Wide Web**. We probably never stop to think about how the Web was invented. In fact, the World Wide Web was invented in 1989 by Tim Berners-Lee.

TOP TIP

Tim gave this advice for building your own website: 'You can link to any piece of information. You don't need to ask for permission. What you create is limited only by your imagination.'

The crowd roared as Tim's tweet was spelled out in lights in the London Olympic Stadium.

The World Wide Web is a vast **network** of documents that are stored on computers around the world. The documents can contain words, pictures and videos. We can view any of these documents on devices such as computers, **tablets** and **smartphones**. **Hyperlinks** connect the documents to each other: when we click on a link we move instantly from one webpage to another.

Tim Berners-Lee could have used his invention to make himself fabulously rich. Instead, he made his idea available to everyone for free. This was why he was honoured with an invitation to appear in the 2012 Olympic opening ceremony. And this was the meaning of his tweet: 'This is for everyone'.

Today Tim Berners-Lee lectures on how the World Wide Web can be used for the good of everyone.

WOW!

Tim Berners-Lee created the world's first website on 6 August 1991. Its address was http://info.cern.ch/hypertext/WWW/TheProject.html. You can still see a version of the site at that address today. By the end of 2014, there were 1 billion websites.

Cardboard computer

Timothy Berners-Lee was born in London on 8 June 1955. He soon had two little brothers, Peter and Michael, and a sister, named Helen. His family lived in a quiet London suburb called East Sheen.

INSPIRATION

Tim's mother was one of the world's first **commercial** computer programmers at a time when women struggled to be treated equally at work. At Ferranti, she successfully fought for women to get the same pay as men.

Tim's parents, Mary and Conway Berners-Lee, were mathematicians. They met in Manchester in 1953, when they were working on the Ferranti Mark 1 computer. The Ferranti Mark 1 was the world's first computer to actually go on sale. Around nine machines were bought by large organizations.

Mary was a programmer, so her job was to give the Mark 1 its instructions. Like computers today, the Mark 1 stored its instructions as **binary numbers** – a series of 0's and 1's. Any information can be put into this form, called digital. The numbers take the form of electrical signals: with a 1 the electricity is switched on and with a 0 it is switched off. But the Mark 1 was very different from today's computers, because it read its instructions from long rolls of paper tape, punched with holes for the 1's.

The Ferranti Mark 1 was 5 m (17 ft) long and 2.7 m (9 ft) high. It was so heavy that the floor underneath it had to be reinforced.

As soon as their children could talk, Mary and Conway passed on their fascination with maths. Anything could be turned into a mathematical game, from measuring the ingredients for a cake to working out the size of a frill on Helen's skirt. 'The whole point about mathematics in our house was that it was fun,' Tim remembers. One of Tim's earliest memories is visiting his dad's office, where he fell in love with the giant computers. Back at home, he built his own pretend computer from cardboard boxes and rolls of old computer tape.

TOP TIP

When Tim was little, his family did not have a television, so they entertained themselves by making, reading and playing. His advice is to do the same: 'As I tell my children, watching television drains your brain out with a small plug.'

The Mark 1 was fed instructions from tape punched with five rows of holes. A row of smaller 'feed holes' ran down the centre.

A banana skins itself

When Tim was little, the Berners-Lee home was a busy, noisy place. The four children joked about puzzles and games. Tim's favourite activity was to raid the scrap materials box for washing-up bottles and springs to build models.

When Tim was four, he started at the local school, Sheen Mount Primary. He was eager to understand how everything around him worked, from electricity to rainbows. He soon became firm friends with a boy called Nicholas Barton. Like Tim, Nick was fascinated by science. The boys encouraged each other to read encyclopaedias and report their findings at playtime.

WOW!

Tim learnt to read before starting school. On the way to Richmond Park, he used to run his fingers over the big letters on street signs. That was how he learnt his letters and how they link to make words.

At weekends, the Berners-Lees went to see the deer in nearby Richmond Park. When it was sunny, they took a picnic.

One day the boys came across *The Book of Experiments* by Leonard de Vries. It was filled with experiments that could be carried out at home, with magical titles such as 'A banana skins itself', 'The tightrope-dancing bottle' and 'The riddle of the hovering ping-pong ball'. At the weekends, Tim, Nick and their friend Christopher carried them out, learning about concepts like air pressure and forces. Tim wanted to dig his own underground laboratory in the back garden, but of course he wasn't allowed.

Eventually, Conway and Mary decided the family would buy a television, as long as they didn't sit around watching it for too long. Tim's favourite programme was *Doctor Who*. His heart beat fast with excitement when it was time for the show. The stories about the time-travelling Doctor and his amazing gadgets fired his imagination – anything was possible!

INSPIRATION

Today, Tim's friend Nicholas Barton is an evolutionary biologist. He studies how species (like humans or dogs) change over millions of years.

In the 1960s, Doctor Who (played here by William Hartnell) used much simpler sets and costumes than science fiction shows do today.

Whistling trains

In 1966, it was time for Tim to go to secondary school. He sat the entrance exam for the prestigious Emanuel School, which was in a different part of London. His parents were delighted when he was offered a place. Tim was worried because all his friends were going to a local school.

Tim built a model railway in his bedroom, complete with a station and tunnels.

INSPIRATION

Tim loved reading science fiction stories by Arthur C. Clarke. One of his favourites was 'Dial F for Frankenstein' about a telephone network that gets a mind of its own and takes over the world's electronic systems.

One of Tim's worries about the new school was the journey: every morning and afternoon, he had to take the train on his own. Emanuel School itself is sandwiched between two train lines. Soon the worry turned into a fascination with trains. Tim got friendly with a group of boys who also liked trainspotting. His parents bought him an electric train set to play with. But Tim was not content to just play: he had to make things happen.

It was the **electronics** of the trains that interested him. He took them apart to see how they worked. Then he constructed electronic gadgets to make the trains stop and start. He wanted to make his trains whistle. By trial and error, he worked out how to wire two **transistors** back to back so that they would make a whistling sound.

Tim's favourite subjects at school were maths and **physics**. Physics is the branch of science that studies the nature of matter and energy. He enjoyed it because – like electronics – it could be put to practical use. When they were old enough, Tim and his close friends went hill-walking during the holidays, staying overnight in youth hostels.

WOW!

One day, Tim was in the living room, using a soldering iron to melt together two pieces of metal. His mother raced out of the kitchen – but rather than tell him off, she showed him how to do it properly.

Tim hated playing rugby and cricket at Emanuel School, but he did enjoy rowing for the school team.

Do it yourself

When he was 18, Tim started a degree in physics at the Queen's College, part of Oxford University. Tim worked hard during his three years at Oxford, but he also got into a bit of trouble.

Tim and his college friends liked to sit around chatting and listening to records. Sometimes Tim played his guitar for everyone. His favourite songs were by a famous singer called Ralph McTell. As time went by, Tim grew close to another physics student, Jane Northcote. The pair became boyfriend and girlfriend.

Tim and his friend Pete started to help organize Rag Week, a series of fun events to raise money for charity. The university had just one computer room, with one printer in it, which could be used only for important work. Tim and Pete sneaked in to print out a heap of information for Rag Week. Just as they were doing so, the computer system crashed, causing panic – the boys got caught and were banned from ever using the university computers again.

The Queen's College was founded in 1341 and named in honour of Queen Philippa, wife of King Edward III.

THE QUEEN'S COLLEGE

Several students at the Queen's College have become famous scientists, including:
- Edmond Halley (1656–1742), the astronomer after whom Halley's comet is named
- Edwin Hubble (1889–1953), the astronomer after whom the Hubble Space Telescope is named

WOW!

Tim was still friends with Nick, who was studying at Cambridge University. One day, when the Oxford tiddlywinks team was driving over to play the Cambridge team, Tim joined the team in order to get a lift.

Computers were expensive, so for Tim there was only one solution: he would build his own. For the keyboard, he adapted a calculator keypad he found in a bin. For the monitor, he paid £5 for the screen from a broken TV set. **Microprocessors** had recently gone on sale. A microprocessor is a small electronic device that acts as the 'brain' of a modern computer, storing instructions and processing information. Tim saved up for a microprocessor using wages from his holiday job in a sawmill. By the time he graduated from Oxford with a first-class degree, he had built his own working computer.

Stepping into the world

In 1976, Tim had a big decision to make: should he continue with his studies or step into the world of work? To Tim, knowledge was not entirely useful until it was put to practical use. He decided to get a job.

The world's first ready-to-use PC was the Apple II. Here it is running a game called 'Ali Baba and the Forty Thieves'.

The world of computers was at an exciting turning point. The arrival of technology such as microprocessors meant that computers no longer had to be huge, expensive machines. The world's first personal computers (PCs) were going on sale to ordinary people. Tim took a job that used his knowledge of computers, at an electronics and computing company called Plessey on England's south coast. Jane also took a job at Plessey and the pair soon got married.

TOP TIP

Tim's advice for programming is to let loose your imagination: 'If you can imagine a computer doing something, you can program a computer to do that.'

THE BIRTH OF PERSONAL COMPUTERS

- 1973: The Xerox Alto is the first computer to be used with a mouse.
- 1977: Apple Computers sells the first ready-to-use personal computer, the Apple II.
- 1983: Microsoft brings out the easy-to-use word-processing program Word.

CERN (in the foreground) is on the outskirts of Geneva, close to the Jura Mountains.

At work, Tim often 'ummed' and 'ahed' when he spoke. He was embarrassed by his terrible memory for people's names and faces. But Tim loved connecting with other people so he made friends easily. He began to become an expert in programming computer **software**. Hardware is the name for the physical parts of a computer, such as the screen and microprocessor. Software is all the **programs** that can run on a computer, instructing it to perform tasks like saving data to the memory or playing a game.

By the late 1970s, Jane and Tim had grown apart, so they decided to divorce. Tim felt he needed a complete change. A friend told him about a job at the European Organization for Nuclear Research, known as CERN, in Switzerland. He jumped at the chance – and got the job.

A day in the life

In 1980, Tim took a six-month job at CERN. CERN is a giant physics laboratory where scientists from around the world carry out experiments into the nature of **atoms** and the tiny particles inside them.

MILESTONES OF THE INTERNET

- 1969: ARPANET is developed for the US Department of Defense. It is a network of computers linking four US universities.
- 1972: The first email is sent over ARPANET.
- 1974: The word 'Internet' is first used as networks around the world start to merge into one giant network, using thousands of kilometres of cables.

Tim was one of the 5000 scientists and programmers working at CERN.

On a typical day at CERN, Tim got to work early. He was programming the system that ran one of the particle accelerators. A particle accelerator speeds up particles then allows them to collide to see if they make new particles. Like most people at CERN in 1980, Tim did not have a computer on his desk.

When Tim needed to program, he went to the central computer control room. Some scientists brought their own computers to CERN, but these were not linked together by wires to form a network. This meant that information could not be sent between computers. No one was linked to the **Internet**.

Information was usually stored only in people's heads. To get a clear idea of what the scientists needed, Tim and his colleagues would grab a coffee and gather round a table at the crossroads of two corridors. 'Discussions at CERN would invariably be accompanied by diagrams of circles and arrows scribbled on napkins and envelopes,' Tim remembers.

At lunchtime, Tim and the team discussed their ideas while gazing at the beautiful view of the Swiss vineyards. They often worked late into the evening.

The Super Proton Synchrotron particle accelerator started work at CERN in 1976. It is in a circle 2 km (1.3 miles) across and is kept in a deep tunnel.

Enquire within upon everything

There were thousands of scientists at CERN, working on different but connected projects. CERN was like a vast, complicated web. With his poor memory for names and faces, how could Tim make sense of it?

INSPIRATION

When Tim was a child, his father explained that computers could only make connections linearly (in a line from A to B) but that if they could make connections in all directions they would be much more powerful.

Tim decided to write a program to help himself remember all the people and projects. He needed to build a database: an organized collection of information. But Tim also wanted to remember the connections between things: someone called Helen wrote a program, which someone called Didier used.

Enquire within upon Everything *is a Victorian encyclopaedia of domestic life, covering everything from dinner parties to weddings.*

Tim knew that our brains work by making connections. For example, a smell can connect his mind to a memory: 'When I smell coffee, strong and stale, I may find myself again in a small room over a corner coffeehouse in Oxford.' Could he write a program that worked like the brain, linking one piece of information to another?

Tim's answer was a program he called ENQUIRE. He named it after a book he loved as a child, called *Enquire within upon Everything*. The book had seemed to be a doorway to the world of information – which made it a perfect name for his program.

ENQUIRE had pages of information called 'cards' and could create links between cards. But ENQUIRE had its limits. It was not designed to run across a network, so other people could not add to it. When Tim left CERN after his six months were up, the disk on which he stored ENQUIRE was lost.

TOP TIP

Tim's advice for learning about any subject is to see the importance of connections: 'The brain has no knowledge until connections are made.'

While he was working at CERN in 1980, Tim wrote ENQUIRE to help with his own poor memory.

Two proposals

Tim spent the next four years working in England, but by 1984 he was looking for a new challenge. He returned to CERN, where he knew there was exciting work still to be done.

Gradually, CERN was equipping everyone with computers, which were being linked into a network. In 1989, CERN finally connected to the Internet, which meant that messages and documents could be sent to and from the world's 1 million Internet users. However, there was still no really useful way for people at CERN to share information about their projects.

In March 1989, Tim proposed a solution to his bosses. His idea was to create a system like ENQUIRE but to allow everyone to read it and add to it using the Internet. Tim proposed using **hypertext** to create links between different pages of information.

INSPIRATION

Robert Cailliau was Tim's friend and colleague at CERN. He was immediately convinced by Tim's proposal and did vital work to persuade their bosses.

Robert Cailliau is a Belgian computer scientist.

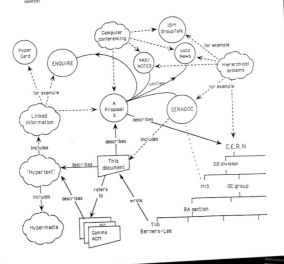

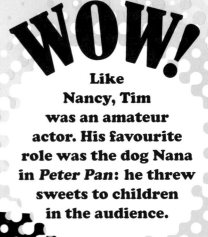

A copy of Tim's proposal for an 'Information Management' system. His boss Mike Sendall has written on it: 'Vague but exciting...'

WOW!

Like Nancy, Tim was an amateur actor. His favourite role was the dog Nana in *Peter Pan*: he threw sweets to children in the audience.

This museum display shows the computer Tim used at CERN, with his proposal *and* Enquire within upon Everything *in front of it.*

Hypertext is text that contains hyperlinks. Hyperlinks are underlined or differently coloured words. When we click on a hyperlink, we are connected to a related page. Hypertext was not a new idea, but Tim was the first person to propose marrying the Internet with hypertext. Tim waited anxiously to see if his proposal would be accepted.

Tim made another proposal in 1989. One evening he had watched a performance by a group of **amateur** actors, one of whom was an American called Nancy Carlson. Nancy was also a computer programmer. When she was younger, she had been a champion figure skater. Tim asked Nancy to marry him.

The first website

In 1990, Tim began two amazing new chapters in his life. He and Nancy got married. His boss, Mike Sendall, allowed him to try out his new system. But what should Tim call it?

In 1990, Tim and his team created the rules that govern how websites are transported across the Internet and displayed on our screens.

Tim knew that his system could change the way people shared ideas – not just at CERN but in the whole world. He wanted a name that suggested the web of connections between ideas and people. Robert Cailliau approved of the name: 'Tim proposes World Wide Web. I like this very much, except that it is difficult to pronounce in French.'

WOW!

On New Year's Eve 1990, Tim and Nancy drove through a whirling snowstorm to the hospital in Geneva. In the early hours of 1991, their daughter Alice was born.

Tim and his team started to produce a hypertext document that people would be able to read using the Internet. It would be the world's first website. The key was to create the new system so it could be used by anyone, anywhere – so Tim needed to set some rules.

First of all, Tim created a language for writing hypertext. He called it **Hypertext Markup Language,** or HTML. In order for people to view websites on their own computers, he needed to make rules for sending hypertext documents over the Internet. He called these rules **Hypertext Transport Protocol**, or HTTP.

Tim also needed a system of addresses to identify websites, like houses are identified by a street name and number. Each website would be given a **Uniform Resource Locator,** or URL. By August 1991, Tim and his team had finished their website, giving it the URL http://info.cern.ch. The first part of the URL (http) tells us that it is a hypertext document. The next part (info.cern) is the **domain name**. It tells us that the computer hosting the website is at CERN. The last part of the URL is the **suffix**. It tells us about the nature or location of the organization that owns the computer. In this case, ch is the suffix for Switzerland.

http://info.cern.ch/hypertext/WWW/T The World Wide We… ×

World Wide Web

The WorldWideWeb (W3) is a wide-area hypermedia information retrieval initiative aiming to give univer

Everything there is online about W3 is linked directly or indirectly to this document, including an executive Frequently Asked Questions .

What's out there?
    Pointers to the world's online information, subjects , W3 servers, etc.
Help
    on the browser you are using
Software Products
    A list of W3 project components and their current state. (e.g. Line Mode ,X11 Viola , NeXTStep , Se
Technical
    Details of protocols, formats, program internals etc
Bibliography
    Paper documentation on W3 and references.
People
    A list of some people involved in the project.
History
    A summary of the history of the project.
How can I help ?
    If you would like to support the web..

Tim's website explained how the Web could work. The URL of the page is in the address bar at the top.

SUFFIXES

• .org means the organization is not profit-making
• .gov means the website is hosted by a government
• .co.uk means the website is hosted by a UK company
• .com means the company is based in the USA or is worldwide

Going global

Tim's computer at CERN was the world's first Web **server**: a computer that stores webpages. But for someone to view the website, they needed to be linked to the Internet and have a **browser**.

A browser is a program that allows computers to read websites. When we type a Web address into our browser, it uses Hypertext Transport Protocol to ask that Web server to send the hypertext file to our computer. The browser then follows the instructions in the Hypertext Markup Language to display the website on our screen.

A browser allows us to surf the Web. If we know the address of the website we are looking for, we can type it in the browser's address bar.

If you've got a tricky project, find motivation the same way as Tim: 'I think the excitement of solving problems motivates me. Working with other people, the excitement of doing things together.'

Tim had created a browser in 1990, but it only worked on his own model of computer. The following year, his colleague Nicola Pellow designed a basic browser that could be used by a range of computers. Tim wanted the Web to spread around the world, so his team released the browser for free, along with instructions on how to set up a website.

Tim would have liked browsers to let users write and edit websites as well as read them, but that idea never took off.

Slowly, scientists at other institutions took an interest. However, they needed a better browser if the Web was really going to take off. Tim suggested that university computer students have a go at designing browsers. By 1993, several groups had designed workable browsers, and about 50 servers were hosting websites.

The breakthrough came in 1994, when the browser Netscape Navigator was released by a team led by American Marc Andreessen. The browser was easy to use and soon made Andreessen a multimillionaire. Tim knew there was no stopping the Web now. But he and Nancy were even more overjoyed by another arrival in 1994: their son Ben.

The Consortium

Tim toyed with the idea of starting a company to make money out of the growing Web. However, what he really wanted was to make sure the Web grew in all the right directions.

Tim started to discuss setting up a group to oversee the Web, sponsored by the famous Massachusetts Institute of Technology (MIT) in the USA. In September 1994, Tim and his family moved to Massachusetts so that he could lead the World Wide Web Consortium, or W3C for short.

WOW!

The first commercial **Internet service providers (ISPs)** were set up in 1989. They give us access to the Internet by cable, phone or wireless links. In 1989, there were around 1 million Internet users; today there are almost 3 billion.

Tim gives a speech about his vision for the Web.

Tim's children Alice and Ben have followed their parents into scientific careers.

W3C has over 300 members, including universities, government bodies and companies that make money from the Web, such as Google and Microsoft. The motto of W3C is 'Leading the Web to its full potential'. Tim and the team make sure that standards, such as HTTP, are met, so that the Web can be used by everyone.

One of Tim's goals is to turn the Web into the Semantic Web. At the moment, computers allow us to read the Web but it's us – people – who make sense of the information on it. The plan for the Semantic Web is to design websites so that computers themselves can 'make sense' of them. For example, if you wanted a book about Manchester United, you could ask your computer not only to search the Web for one, but to decide which book is cheapest and place an order for you. Many of the tools needed for the Semantic Web are still being developed, so it will be years before it is fully functioning.

HONOURS BOARD

• 1999: Tim is named as one of *Time* magazine's 100 Most Important People of the 20th Century.
• 2004: Tim receives a knighthood from the Queen, making him 'Sir' Berners-Lee.
• 2012: He is made a member of the international Internet Hall of Fame.

W3C's head office is in a MIT building designed by the architect Frank Gehry.

A world wide change

Many people think the Web has the power to change the way we live more than any invention the world has yet seen – more than the steam engine, the light bulb or the telephone. It has already changed the way we study, work and communicate.

If Tim had not invented the Web, someone else would have done. But if that inventor had been more interested in making money than sharing ideas, the Web would not be free. Although we usually pay for an Internet service provider, we never pay to surf the Web. That is why the Web has worked its way into our lives.

Girls surf the Web on a tablet in a cybercafé in Senegal, Africa. Only about 1 in every 5 people in Africa has Internet access, but that number is growing.

WOW!

Tim campaigns to keep the Web free from interference by governments and businesses, so that all our voices can be heard equally.

The Web can show us what is happening on the other side of the world as it happens. If we see injustice, we can use the Web to campaign for change. The Web allows people to form friendships across distances. We can buy products without leaving the house. We can use an online encyclopaedia to complete a school project.

The Web is for everyone, so we all have responsibility for it. Some of us are less responsible than others, so we must take care that what we read and watch on the Web is decent and honest. As Tim says: 'The technology allows humanity to express itself and interact. If you are frightened of it then you are frightened of what humanity can do.'

Tim wants the Web to be a force for good – and we all need to play a part.

WEB MILESTONES

- 1995: Amazon, the world's largest online shop, is founded.
- 1997: The Google **search engine** is launched.
- 2001: The free online encyclopaedia Wikipedia is set up.
- 2004: Facebook, a **social networking** service, goes online.

Anyone can set up their own website to share ideas and skills.

Have you got what it takes to be an inventor?

1) Are maths and science your favourite subjects in school?
a) I love those subjects so much that I even do puzzles and experiments at home.
b) I enjoy them most of the time, but it depends what the lesson is about.
c) I am more excited by other subjects, like athletics, writing or art.

2) Do you like finding out how things work?
a) I am always asking questions and borrowing books from the library to find out more.
b) I really enjoy it when my teachers or parents explain new ideas to me.
c) I don't often think about how gadgets work.

3) Do you enjoy the challenge of hard work? How do you feel when you are given a difficult homework project?
a) I am never put off by hard work, so I get straight down to any new project.
b) I don't mind hard work, but I get tired if a project is too difficult.
c) I am happy to work hard if I can pull in my skills, like drawing pictures or interviewing people.

4) Do you enjoy solving problems?
a) I know there's a solution to every problem and it's just a question of finding it.
b) Sometimes I don't know where to start when I'm faced with a difficult problem.
c) I love helping my friends when they tell me about their problems.

5) Are you good at listening to other people's ideas? Are you happy to work in a team when the task demands it?
a) I know my own mind, but I still enjoy working with other people.
b) I worry that my voice gets drowned out when I work in a team.
c) I enjoy working with people much more than working with computers.

6) When you're older, would you like to use your skills to make the world a better place?
a) I already have plans that will change the world.
b) I'd love to get a job that makes a difference to the world.
c) I don't know exactly what I want to do yet, but I know it will be exciting.

RESULTS

Mostly As: You've got what it takes to be an inventor: vision, determination and a love of learning. Keep up the good work!

Mostly Bs: You could be anything you want – as long as you have the determination to reach your goals. Try building your self-confidence by pursuing a range of interests.

Mostly Cs: You have lots of different skills so you know it's too early to decide what you want to be. Just keep on learning and enjoying everything you do.

Glossary

amateur Unpaid; just for fun.

atoms The smallest parts of a chemical element (such as oxygen or gold).

binary numbers A system of representing numbers using only 0's and 1's. For example, 1 = 1, 2 = 10, 3 = 11, 4 = 100, 5 = 101, 6 = 110.

browser A program that allows us to read websites.

commercial Aiming to make a profit.

domain name A unique name that identifies a website or other Internet service.

electronics The use of electrical circuits.

hyperlinks Links to another page or portion of text. Readers can follow links by clicking a mouse, pressing a key or touching a screen.

hypertext Text, pictures and videos that contain hyperlinks. Hypertext is displayed on a computer or other electronic device.

Hypertext Markup Language (HTML) The computer language in which most websites are written.

Hypertext Transport Protocol (HTTP) Rules for transporting hypertext over the Internet.

Internet A worldwide network of computer networks. Computers communicate across the Internet by sending information in packets.

Internet service providers (ISPs) Organizations that give us access to the Internet by cable, phone line or wireless link.

microprocessors Small electronic devices that act as the 'brain' of modern computers.

network A group of connected people or things. A computer network is made up of computers connected by cables or wireless links.

physics The branch of science that studies the nature of matter and energy.

programs Sets of instructions that allow a computer to perform tasks.

search engine A program that searches for sites on the Web.

server A Web server is a computer or group of computers that stores and delivers webpages.

smartphones Mobile phones that include a computer, browser and wireless technology.

social networking Web services that allow people to connect with others who have similar interests.

software The programs used by a computer.

suffix A domain name suffix is the last part of the unique name that identifies a website. Common examples are .com and .org.

tablets Small portable computers that have touchscreens rather than keyboards or mice.

transistors Electronic devices that can switch or increase the strength of electric current.

tweet Short message on the Twitter website.

Uniform Resource Locator (URL) Address of a location on the Internet, such as a website.

websites Sets of connected pages on the Web, created by a particular person or group.

wireless Communicating without connecting wires, often using radio waves.

World Wide Web A worldwide network of hypertext files, which we can access using the Internet.

Index